Healing Chi

Meditation

By

William Lee

Author of Amazon Bestsellers:

5-Minute Chi Boost

5- Minute Stress Management

T.A.E. Total Attack Elimination

Happy & Gluten Free

Chi Healing Powers Book Set

Total Self Defense Book Set

&

Total Chi Fitness

Acknowledgments:

To my students and friends. You are all selflessly helping me.

Special thanks to those who asked, insisted, and assisted me in turning the seminars into this book.

Costumer Reviews

By WONDERPIEL

I've always been eager to know about the different ways of mental and physical exercises. Being a health conscious person, I spend most of my leisure time in researching about the ways and techniques of Yoga and meditation. I have a fit athletic body and I daily attend my gym sessions.

I came to know about this book through a friend at gym. He told me about the Chinese ways of meditation, techniques to control flow of breath and stress. They can help me to cover my exercising needs. I have read other books of William Lee and have learnt a lot from them. I used to have sinus problem but successfully recovered it through the Chi-fitness techniques. The book has all the basic and simple styles, I recommend those for the beginners as they can easily practice them.

The author wants his readers to maintain cleanliness in order to produce mental and physical stretchiness. I also saw the video of total Chi fitness and learned new meditation methods. No wonder Chinese people are counted amongst the most active people of the world, they practice Yoga and deep meditation exercises.

Healing Chi meditations are the best for people facing chronic diseases. They will instantly feel energetic and will recover in no time. I will definitely suggest the Yoga practitioners to try this book and stay healthy throughout their lives. I wasn't expecting such a smooth flow of writing but overall, the language was understandable and simple. Adapt the Chinese way of living to acquire thousands of health benefits! Cheers!

By Brian McFamo

Chi: the force from within. This book literally is a game changer. Healing with Chi meditation not only is sleek, but it is innovative. It literally shows you step by step, easy to follow method to healing the mind body and soul! sifu William Lee has done it and I would recommend this book to anyone seeking to channel their chi!

By Janja

Healing Chi Meditation (Chi Powers for Modern Age) is a great informative guide that explains in a simple way everything you need to know about Chi meditation. You will learn everything, from the basics of Chi energy to detailed explanation about practicing Chi meditation. You will find out why it is so important for your general well-being and how you can achieve it. It will help you if you suffer from lack of energy, headaches, problems with concentration, physical weakness, mental weakness, low energy levels, depression, emotional problems,...just to name a few.

It brings so many benefits that it's definitely worth it to try, so I highly recommend this great book if you want to do something good for yourself and your health.

TABLE OF CONTENTS:

Introduction

I'll admit that it was a mistake to leave out an explanation of Chi meditation techniques in my previous books. Why do I say that? Quite simply, I received far too many emails with questions and inquiries about how to practice Chi meditation. I have answered each email and letter, explaining some of the reasons behind my decision, and this book should provide more details for those who are really interested. In case you are thinking of skipping this introduction, let me explain what this book is all about, and what are the results of methods that I teach.

"Your health (physical, mental, and emotional) will be molded into a natural and harmonious form. Chi meditation will rejuvenate your existence on all levels. All that is around us and everything within us is driven by Chi. The causes of pain, disease, and discomfort will melt away, along with all that stops you living life to your full potential. All blockages will disappear and you will feel the freedom and power of living in harmony with Chi and the universe."

Is this is something that you find interesting? I promise you right now, this is real and achievable. It can become your reality as well.

Only for the Sick and Weak?

Healing Chi Meditation is not meant ONLY for the sick, diseased, and weak - yet at the same time, it is. Who has perfect health nowadays? Today, enjoying complete health on all levels is rarely found. If you are on that level, congratulations! It's true that even advanced Healing Chi Meditation practitioners must make concerted efforts and continue practicing in order to maintain that kind of level.

Anyone in need of healing can benefit greatly from these methods, though the manifestations of pain, disease, and sickness shouldn't be the only reasons for one to begin with Healing Chi Meditation. We can (and we should) always enhance our activities and performance, to improve our lives.

Why This Book?

This book contains practical and easily applicable Chi Meditation techniques that have benefited many lives for thousands of years, regardless of any material or spiritual factors. If you practice these techniques correctly, *they will* benefit your life immensely.

This book isn't at all theoretical. Since we are not face-to-face and I can't directly teach you these methods, this book contains all of the necessary information for one who desires to master the Healing Chi Meditation methods. This book can be useful regardless of any belief, philosophy, or religion held by the reader.

This work is a *Chi Meditation User Manual,* and may seem too short to some people. I wanted to offer a short practical guidebook that anyone could use right away. It contains all of the elements, details, and advice about Chi energy meditation understanding and application.

Priorities

After almost forty years of teaching Chi Kung and martial arts in the Western world, I've got plenty of ways to confirm the absolutely practical nature of what I have learned from my *Sifu* (teacher). One of those truths is that Chi Meditation works better for most people when used alongside good lifestyle choices. Let me explain: Chi Meditation is very powerful and can benefit anyone. However, there are factors that are favorable and those that aren't. The results of Healing Chi Meditation techniques are influenced by common-sense factors such as a healthy lifestyle, level of health, and a positive mindset.

Healing Chi Meditation is about cleaning and restructuring your life energy ("Chi"). The methods of this book will be much more effective and beneficial if your diet, lifestyle, and mindset aim towards positivity and health. For that reason, I published my teachings about Chi Kung applications before publishing this manual for Healing Chi Meditation.

Misinterpretation

Currently, people are overwhelmed by the variety and amount of information about 'anything and everything'. Neither Chi nor meditation methods are an exception to this trend. Unfortunately, this doesn't create a beneficial environment for serious individuals about a proper and complete approach to Chi Meditation. One has to know whose advice is worth the effort and time of making lifestyle changes. Shiny advertisements, book covers, and commercials created to influence our minds aren't easy to ignore or see beyond. People are more or less helpless if they rely solely on superficial advice and information from media sources (and marketing channels that control the media).

However, I know from experience that serious people interested in reality (and not mesmerized by attractive packaging) are able to recognize real value when they see it. Despite Healing Chi Meditation's presentation of higher knowledge, I decided to cover the 'physical' approach to Chi Kung in my previous books (http://www.amazon.com/William-Lee/e/B00DWFOCV8), in order to differentiate them from countless numbers of esoteric, new age, religious and other meditation-related books out there. I have nothing against philosophy and theories but I dislike the cheaters and speculators. The discipline of working with Chi can show measurable, practical, and applicable outcomes, as shown in the Healing Chi Meditation exercises explained in this book. One shouldn't expect any other result.

Chapter I. - Basics

1. What Is (and What Isn't) Chi Energy?

Ancient books from various cultures around the world offer explanations related to using and manipulating *life energy* or *life force*. Like most of you, I couldn't find the time to study all of the different traditions, though I have learned some basic principles shared by most traditions.

Different traditions understand and work with the subject of *'energy that powers everything'* in a fairly similar way, though some are more useful and practical for the lifestyles of modern men and women. Let's review the facts that are most important to know in order to ensure the successful application of the Healing Chi Meditation program. (If you have already been introduced to the basic facts about Chi energy, you may decide to skip over these next few paragraphs, though I have learned that there is nothing wrong in repeating the important and basic elements of anything.) So, here is a short summary of the most important facts about Chi:

- Chi (or 'Qi') is a Chinese term used to describe the vital force that is present everywhere. It is the moving energy of everything. Without the presence of Chi, no sign of life could be seen.

- Chi, 'energy of life' or 'life force', is addressed differently in various philosophies and cultures; Ki in Japan, Prana in India, Mana in Hawaiian culture, Lüng in Tibetan Buddhism, etc. All of those terms refer to the same vital energy of life.

- In nature, as well as as in our bodies, Chi energy is constantly circling and flowing, supplying life force to each and every limb, muscle and organ – to every single cell of our body and mind.

- Inside our body, Chi flows via subtle energy channels known as 'meridians'. There are a few main energy pathways and many pressure points situated along these energy paths.

- Whenever there is a situation that makes a healthy flow of Chi weaker or disturbed, we start feeling a certain discomfort, tension, pain, etc. Our body is being forced by Chi (or lack of Chi) to focus our attention on the existence of a problem.

- By proper treatment (using various pressure points, breathing and posture, or meditation), one can efficiently revive the healthy and strong flow of a 'life force' in our bodies. That is the essence of health.

This Healing Chi Meditation practice is not difficult to understand, nor is it reserved for a 'special' group of people. Everyone who decides to do so can successfully learn the Healing Chi Meditation techniques regardless of beliefs, age, education, sex, or any other material condition.

Money, fame, good looks, or intelligence cannot help anyone to become 'better' in the art of Chi meditation. In order to quickly get the results of Healing Chi Meditation, you do not need any sort of material qualification. It's all about your willingness to learn, feel, and work with Chi.

These are the most basic and important facts that we must know in order to begin. When we really decide to do something, sooner or later we will end up doing/having/experiencing exactly what we decided.

Therefore, my only question to you is this:

'Are you serious about learning Chi meditation? How serious are you about improving your health and well-being?'

Please stop reading for a moment. Before continuing, why not answer my question – even if only in your head? Try it, please. I do not need your answer - but you do! If you are alone while reading this, you can even answer aloud. If you have a mirror nearby (a mobile camera reverse option works just fine), that's even better - just look deep into your own eyes and simply answer this question. No one else needs to hear your answer but you! You need to become clear on this – believe it or not, this step is very important for your success. If your answer is positive and you are clear about it, you will advance much faster. If you are not sure that you will give these Healing Chi Meditation methods a fair chance, you can't be sure about the results either.

This is not a 'responsibility transfer' attempt or a disclaimer. This is a simple fact of life. In the same way that you "can lead a horse to water but you can't make it drink", I cannot make this decision for you. The best thing is that you can!

If you decide to give this book enough attention, and you try out these techniques seriously, you will be very, very happy with the outcome.

2. Empty Cup

Before answering this question ('Why should I consider doing Chi meditation?'), I think you will find it useful to address a point that is at least as important. Decide for yourself. Some readers of this book will not know much about Chi energy or internal skills. For them, I hope that this book will serve as solid introduction. Other readers will be familiar with, or even very experienced, in some method of working with life force. To those who know something of Chi energy, I ask you to consider this parable.

There is an old Taoist story about a young man who comes to a master asking to become his student. After a while, the old and wise master invites him over for a cup of tea. The master listens to the young man's questions and begins to reply. However, every time the master starts to explain a point, the young man interrupts him by saying something like this:

"Oh I understand, I actually do (this) when (that) occurs..."

"Yes, exactly! I don't act like that because...."
etc.

Very soon the wise master stopped speaking, and began looking directly at the teapot. He then started pouring tea into the cup in front of the young man. In a few moments the cup was filled with Jasmine tea, but the master didn't stop. Before the young man could react or say anything, hot tea overflowed onto the table in front of him and started dripping everywhere.

The young man jumped up from his seat and yelled:

"Master, stop! It's enough, my cup is full! Can't you see?!"

The old master responded with a smile on his face:

"Yes. Your cup is full. I'm not able to teach you anything before you empty your cup. You have to make space for new lessons."

The moral of the story is obvious. Many times we maintain that same unteachable attitude. Our 'teachability index' has to be high and we have to be ready in order to learn something new. If we seriously desire to get the best results out of anything, we had better try to empty our cup and make space for new knowledge and skills.

Yes, I know – it's easier said than done. However, if the desire to learn with an open mind proves to be weaker than our attempts to show how much we already understand and know, we won't gain anything! Just like the young man in the Taoist story who wasn't able to learn anything new, a person that allows his 'teachability index' to remain low can't enjoy the benefits of new insights and skills. It's that simple.

Emptying your cup doesn't imply that you have to neglect all that you have learned. That would be absurd. With this 'empty cup' point, I simply want to indicate the importance of adopting a teachable attitude. That won't deplete anything out of the stock of your personal values, knowledge, and experience. It will just increase the capability and power to enlarge those valuable things. By 're-learning to learn', you are providing the best chance for your personal advancement. Don't misunderstand me. An expert teacher who entirely understands and has progressed in the practical application of what he (or she) teaches, is very important - especially when you want to learn some type of inner skill, such as Chi meditation. The truth is, there are a lot of pitfalls on the path. If unconnected or unguided by a representative of the original knowledge, one can't be sure about the outcome and results. That connection and mentorship will make sure that the learner stays away from pitfalls and obstacles.

3. Chi Meditation - Why?

I may be wrong, but I do think that coming up with an answer to this question is an interesting and necessary step to take before we move forward. Some of you may be already convinced, but others will want to get a clear answer. So, in case you plan to skip over next chapter (I don't advise you do that if you want to get all the details), let me provide you with a quick list of the benefits enjoyed by practitioners of Healing Chi Meditation. You should consider this program in case you suffer through these ailments or you feel these things:

- Lack of energy
- Headaches
- Difficulties in concentration or in maintaining focus
- Physical weakness
- Mental weakness
- Low energy levels
- Need to boost performance in sports
- Need to boost professional performance
- Desire to boost weight loss results
- Need to improve detoxing results
- Chronic pain
- Allergies
- Difficulty living without painkillers and/or

medication
- Need to boost your libido and sex drive
- High or low blood pressure issues
- Depression
- Emotional problems
- Digestion disorders
- Need to accelerate healing after serious illness or surgery

Everyone who has read my previous books will recognize this list. How is this Chi meditation program different? Quite truthfully, it isn't. This Healing Chi Meditation is meant to make Chi flow in a strong, healthy way throughout your body, just like Chi Kung, acupressure, acupuncture, and various other methods. What is different is the method itself. Your body is not moving – this is Chi meditation we speak about. Not Tai Chi, Chi Kung, or any other method that will require you to move your body.

4. Ease of Everyday Life Application

Ease of application is probably the most unique characteristic of the Healing Chi Meditation program. Once you master these simple techniques, you can (and you should) use them whenever you need them. The best part is the fact that we all have plenty of 'dead time' that can be nicely transformed into active and rejuvenating Chi meditation sessions:

Passive traveling (traveling but not driving car, train, tube, bus, airplane ...)
Waiting in line or a queue...
Waiting for someone or something to happen at your workplace ...

You may come up with even more ways and situations where you can apply some Healing Chi Meditation techniques in your everyday life. Keep in mind that we must first understand and learn what are these Healing Chi Meditations, and how to do them properly. Once mastered, you can apply them in all kinds of situations without a problem. Next to having the necessary desire to learn, one just needs a bit of experience and creativity.

Chapter II. – Benefits

There is not enough space in this book to describe the details of each and every possible benefit enjoyed by practitioners of these methods. However, in order to make sure you have enough grounds for making a serious decision to be (and stay) motivated in meditation, I would like to briefly present this subject matter.

1. Physical Health Benefits

As already stated, physical benefits of Chi meditation are numerous. One must also consider that the benefits will vary with the individual. However, some major areas of benefit apply to everyone. These are based on the steps needed to prepare for Chi meditation.

Relaxation

Though it's true that this process is not entirely physical, a great percentage of the effectiveness of Chi meditation is due to physical preparation. The first step in preparing the mind for Chi meditation is to relax as much as possible. The business and concerns of everyday matters distract thoughts and spread them in many directions. Many of these thoughts are wasteful, or they are simply emotions that run a course of their own at times. However, these thoughts and concerns leave physical traces in the body: tensions, taut muscles, and occasional pain. Our bodies and minds can act like coiled springs ready to explode. Chi meditation turns the mind and body toward calm and quiet.

Correct Breathing

Due to the nature of the methods, practitioners are blessed with all of the health benefits of breathing correctly. Correct breathing techniques are the engine for effective meditation. Normal breathing comes from the chest alone. One inhales (expanding the chest) and exhales while dropping the chest. Unfortunately, this typical 'high breathing' is responsible for (or at least an accessory to) a wide variety of physical difficulties.

To prepare for Chi meditation, one needs to learn a new breathing technique called 'diaphragmatic breathing'. Once mastered, this method will pay you dividends in every part of life. Each and every part of your body and mind is influenced by how you breathe. Later chapters will explain the exact method that will help you to learn and switch to proper Chi breathing.

Connection to Universal Energy

Once you get accustomed to Chi meditation and begin to apply it, Chi flow will reestablish its natural paths. All of your inner organs will start functioning properly again, and your brain will be stimulated to new heights.

The Chi meditation philosophy explains that there are energies all around us, from the Earth, from the sun, from food we eat, and from every other living being. When establishing a healthy and strong Chi flow within our body, we connect strongly to energies around us and with the universal field of Chi. After practicing these methods, our ability to receive healthy, clean, and much-needed energy can soon double and triple. Beneficial practices like walking barefoot, swimming in the ocean or river waters, or breathing fresh air, can form entirely new and deeper dimensions of energy for us. Our diseases, pains, and medical conditions can disappear, melted away by clean Chi that we learn to move and absorb from nature and from the universe in general.

Body – Mind Overall Energy Boost

With practice, the use of Healing Chi Meditation leads to a state in which one will feel energy flowing through the body. After a few weeks of proper practice, one will sense a stronger connection between mind and body. In all sorts of physical movements or activities, one should feel added power and balance. Increasing your performance level at sports or work should happen automatically, and can be additionally enhanced by intentionally directing Chi energy in the later stages of Healing Chi Meditation practice.

It's beneficial to know that the universe can speak to one connected with the universal Chi energy flow. If one is in a state of harmony with the universe, pain and discomfort has no business to do. This stage can be achieved in time and without any elaborate steps. Once you are fixed at that stage of universal Chi harmony, it's possible to have health, vigor, and wisdom accompany you throughout the day. Like a reservoir of strength, it can add purpose and greater meaning to every part or aspect of life.

2. Benefits to the Nervous System

When it comes to Chi meditation, numerous benefits accompany it. The thing that you have to keep in mind is that Chi flows primarily through the meridians (energy paths within the gross and subtle body) that are very closely related to the nervous system. It's one of the main reasons why Healing Chi Meditation practitioners feel and enjoy multiple benefits in the nervous system.

Getting In Touch With the Body

Getting in touch with the body is one main thing which Chi Meditation practice helps you to do. If anything is not working well in your body, then Healing Chi Meditation methods will help you to heal it, not only because it adds more Chi to your body, but also because it directs Chi energy to exactly where it needs to go.

Chi meditation works to unblock the flow of Chi within the nervous system. Clearing the blockages in your nervous system will help to strengthen your Chi, which will then be used to help heal the body, and you will feel healthier and happier. Ultimately, you will feel more comfortable in your skin and enjoy some of these benefits that are connected with the nervous system: deep sleep, improved ability to focus, increased concentration, freshness. Many people are especially interested in the next benefit of Healing Chi Meditation.

Stress Relief

The methods of Healing Chi Meditation have been shown to help with various issues and medical conditions connected to stress. For example, you may have heard the term that you are 'nervous', or you just know this to be true about yourself. When you are nervous or stressed out, it can cause damage to the nervous system over a long period of time. Relieving stress is something that will help to reduce this problem. As a result, regenerating the nervous system is something that becomes essential for a healthy life.

One of the final benefits of this Healing Chi Meditation program, when it is directed to the nervous system, is that it helps one to be more present. When your nervous system is unbalanced or out of whack, you will have a much harder time being present because your nervous system will simply not let you. However, when less of your chi is blocked, it becomes easier to experience the world around you moment by moment.

3. Emotional Benefits of Chi Meditation

The beauty of performing Healing Chi Meditation (or Chi Meditation in general) is that virtually anyone can do it. It is not necessary to be in top physical form, to hold any special degree, or to understand complex ideologies. While Chi Meditation is essentially easy to perform, there are ways to prepare yourself for meditation that will enable you to derive the greatest mental and emotional benefits from the practice. Most Westerners practice Chi Meditation as a way to relieve stress, which is a huge factor in heart disease and other physical ailments. Reducing stress is important, but the regular practice of Chi Meditation will also improve other aspects of your physical, emotional, and mental health.

The purpose of Healing Chi Meditation is to empower a practitioner with ways to enter a state of relaxed responsiveness, during the meditation session as well as throughout the waking hours. This can be likened to driving a car so often that you drive safely without even thinking about what you are doing. Essentially, the proper operation of the motor vehicle has become so ingrained in your habits, you can drive anywhere without stress or worry, and you can instantly react to unexpected traffic situations because of your level of mental preparation.

The same principle applies to the regular deliberate practice of Healing Chi Meditation.

Eventually, you will achieve a mindful and meditative mindset throughout your day regardless of any situation. The ability to engage in daily activities and stressful situations while maintaining a serene manner and positive mindset becomes as easy as driving to work on a day without a traffic jam. It is not easy to separate the benefits one receives (on the level of emotions and emotional intelligence) from the benefits described just above in the previous chapter, because they are so closely related. However, one should be aware of the whole new spectrum of emotional skills, which can open up to a serious and regular practitioner. New experiences and the depth of a whole new dimension can unfold before your eyes and within your heart.

Chi Meditation is a method to use if one needs improvement or help with issues such as these:

- Emotional problems
- Empathy
- Patience
- Understanding and feeling for others
- Gratefulness
- Ability to give and receive love

Regular Chi Meditation is calming, when practiced correctly. You should not be on an emotional roller coaster, nor deal with daily issues by having knee-jerk reactions that could have negative emotional and mental consequences for you, your loved ones, or your co-workers.

Chapter III. – How to Prepare

1. External Preparation

Some people think that Chi Meditation presents the same challenges (stilling the mind and focusing) as found in traditional seated meditations such as Taoist or Buddhists methods. While this is not completely factual, the greater truth is that your degree of mastery over these two components directly affects the success of your Chi meditations. More mastery leads to more success.

Preparations are always important, though the early stages of practice will be much more productive if more preparations are taken. Beginning with simple concepts, such as these commonly known ideas, are simply not enough:

"Approach your Chi meditation in a relaxed manner" or

"Calm and center yourself before you begin."

These are good methods, but they don't go far enough. Below are outlined some preparation methods (cleanliness, environment, stretching methods, etc) which should really get a practitioner into the necessary state of mind beyond simple relaxation. However, the amount of preparation that you will apply really depends on your personal preference. My simple point is this: prepare yourself better to get better results, especially in the beginning and during first few months of practice.

Cleanliness

One of the best forms of external preparation, prior to meditation, is to clean yourself in some form of purification. For those who want to go through a thorough preparation ritual, it is important to take a bath or a shower to physically wash away the troubles and dirt of the day. Other forms of 'ritual' cleaning might be brushing one's teeth, shaving, or just washing the hands before sitting down to meditate. How in-depth the process goes depends on how much preparation and focus an individual needs to get his or her mind into the proper frame of reference.

Environment

It is also important to prepare the place in which one will be meditating. This means that individuals need to try their best to minimize any sort of distraction by turning off cell phones, computers (Skype, Facebook etc.), and sources of possible disturbing noises (television). Closing an open door can also be helpful, so that no chatter from the outside world can invade the meditation session. For those who find music to be relaxing, it is a good idea to find tunes that relax the mind and assist with focus. While classical music works for some people, others may prefer the natural sounds of recorded rain, ocean, or night noises (such as bullfrogs and crickets). Turning down the artificial lighting, or opting for a few candles, can also help cut down on distractions. Lastly, some people find lighting incense to be an aid to meditation.

It is important to know that all of these methods are not crucial elements of success, but these ways to prepare yourself for Chi meditation can be necessary for beginners and can have a positive effect on many practitioners' experiences.

Stretching and Exercise

A great panorama of external methods exist to help people prepare for internal meditation. These preparations are largely symbolic, helping the person to make a transition from day-to-day distractions and move into the contemplation of the mental and spiritual realm. The more practice in which a person engages, the less preparation is required to achieve the proper state of mind for successful Chi Meditation.

Many people prefer to go through a small exercise routine before settling down to meditate properly. This might take the form of some basic stretches, or it could be a series of movements meant to center and direct the flow of chi. Whatever kind of exercise one prefers, it needs to work as a way to cast off the worries of the day and to strip away distraction. I personally recommend, and can totally guarantee, the success of the Total Chi Fitness program (https://www.amazon.com/Total-Chi-Fitness-Stretching-Performance-ebook/dp/B00BZG7NK8). By focusing on the movements of the body, the person gets into the proper state of mind to focus on the internal workings of both the mind and the spirit. Again, this step is not required, but it is beneficial for many individuals who need some extra external preparation before meditation. Also, it allows for a stronger flow of Chi, which can promote a sense of calm and focus as much as being in a quiet room without distractions.

My Gift you may find very helpful - Total Chi Fitness exercise routine video, you can get <u>from this link</u> (http://eepurl.com/6JUtP)

Other Factors

Strive to find a time and a place where you will not be interrupted, and allow yourself plenty of time to meditate. (It will certainly <u>not</u> be conducive to relaxation if you have a mental stopwatch ticking away, with a laundry list of errands to complete before the day ends.) Setting aside enough time and guarding against interruptions are the two best things that you can do to ensure a successful meditation session. The more relaxed that you are, the more your central nervous system will benefit. Deep breathing induces calm, and that calming effect then helps you to release stress, thus allowing the chi energy within your body to become balanced.

The ultimate result of an unhurried Chi Meditation session is a calmer, focused mind. In turn, this state of being results in clearer thinking, better decision-making, and an inner assurance and confidence that you can meet all of life's demands. This is not to suggest that during meditation you will experience a dramatic life-changing epiphany, but you will be more relaxed and open to new insights that will affect your daily life in positive ways.

2. **Preparation of the Mind**

Before each Chi Meditation session, take a few moments to think about the enormous benefits which the meditation will bring to you. Imagine for a few moments what your life will look like when you face every day and every situation with a peaceful inner assurance that you are in control of your emotional and mental health. There is no hurry, and you will always reap some benefits, but the benefits will be greater if you do not become anxious about the results or try to force a particular desired outcome.

Chi Meditation is a unique way for people to clear their minds, relax their bodies, and help strengthen their spirits. However, this form of meditation is more than just the activity of sitting in a single position and taking deep breaths. It is important for practitioners, but especially for those who are just learning the art of Chi Meditation, to go through the proper external preparations before settling down to the serious business of Chi Meditation.

Calming the mind is one of the most important areas of meditation preparation. It can be said that an unfettered state of mind is the best state for getting the most out of meditation. Deep breathing exercises might be the most common means in which the mind is calmed for meditation. When the mind is racing, meditation is not going to be possible. Engaging in deep breathing (through the nose and not the mouth) allows someone to calm their mind even if they're not sure how to do it. The process of deep breathing is easy and is a part of Healing Chi Meditation.

Ways to Calm the Mind

Once you are in your preferred meditation position, simply inhale deeply, hold for a second, and exhale slowly. Ten repetitions of this exercise can aid in calming the mind.

An even easier exercise allows sound to calm the mind. In your meditation position, you empty your mind and merely witness a sound you may hear in the background. A bird chirping outside would be perfect. However, do not focus on the chirping because you want your mind to be'empty. Engaging in 'witnessing' means that the sound is acknowledged and allowed to pass. Hence, it offers a calming but not a distracting effect.

In a similar vein, a lit candle can be placed in clear view as you start to meditate. Staring into the candle and simply witnessing the glow and flicker of the flame can help reduce any internal noise. To repeat, try not to concentrate on the flame or think about it. Rather, just witness its sights and sounds and allow the mind to drift slowly into a calm state.

Dressing in comfortable clothing should never be overlooked when attempting to calm the mind. Tight clothing can be distracting, and distractions draw attention. Constant reminders that clothing lacks comfort does not help the cause of calming the mind. Even a light exercise session might, surprisingly, make the mind calmer. Anxiety can certainly upset a calm mind.

Every step for calming the mind may take some practice. With the right effort, the ability to achieve desirable results is possible.

Chapter IV. – Meditation Explained

1. Breathing & Meditation

Aimed at relaxation, the breathing technique clears the mind, provides a healthy supply of oxygen to the brain, and increases focus. However, that's not the whole point. A mind focused on deep breathing via the Healing Chi Meditation process creates a strong Chi energy flow all over the physical and subtle body. Breathing is very important but that's not all there is to Healing Chi Meditation, which reduces mental clutter, then calms the mind, and finally opens the mind.

The goal of meditation, in a sense, is to open up the mind and spirit, and let these parts achieve balance. One can describe the opening of the mind as opening the heart and mind to the universe. Breathing alone will not accomplish this goal.

2. Dan Tian Centering

This is the most important and basic breathing-related exercise that you can do anytime, alongside or separate from other methods described in this chapter. If you have limited time for your Chi Meditation session, I recommend that you stick to this Dan Tian Centering before you move further to learn other methods such as the 8 Moons. These exercises fit very well together but this is more important for a proper beginning.

By practicing these Chi breathing exercises, you not only clear the body and mind from all negative energy (and reactions to stress), but over time, you will develop a habit of using them in everyday life. Your body will automatically switch to these breathing patterns whenever there is a need to fight stress, fear, anxiety, or anything negative. It is the same as with all other things: you must consciously practice at first. As your body and mind experience the relief and blessings of these practices, you will be more and more driven toward them.

It is a natural process. People who use these exercises are soon able to practice them spontaneously in everyday life, as needed.

Technique:

For doing this exercise, it's better to use a sitting or standing position. Avoid lying down, since it isn't a good position for this exercise.

Stage 1 – Discover Your Center

Everything in nature has its center. The triple question is, do we know where to find it, can we see it, and how can we use it for our benefit? The whole essence of this stage is that human bodies have a center of energy. In fact, there are a few energy centers. Chinese scriptures call it "Dan Tian" (tan tien), which literally means "the elixir field". "Elixir" refers to vital Chi energy that has consolidated into a pearl. Hence, Dan Tian refers to a spot in a person's body where his vital energy has accumulated into a field. The most ideal position for storing energy is at the *qi-hai* vital point or the *guan-yuan* vital point, located 2 ½ to about three inches below the naval, not on the surface, but about two inches beneath the surface of the abdomen. Now, pay attention, since people often fail to properly understand this.

The "inch" used here is neither the Chinese measurement nor the British inch, but a "biological inch". (What in the world is a 'biological inch'? Don't worry; it's pretty simple to clarify.) A "biological inch" is the distance between the first and the second joints of the right hand of your index finger.

Just simply measure 2 ½ to three biological inches below your navel. Using your thumb, press that area toward your spine, not too hard but not too soft. You should feel that pressure but it should not be uncomfortable. Keep that pressure on for a minute or two, breathing slowly, focusing on your Dan Tian. This is how to prepare for the next part of Chi Meditation.

Stage 2 - Chi Breathing:

In Chi Meditation, we use the abdominal breathing technique, which is the most effective for this type of program.

Abdominal breathing is a very simple and natural way to breathe - newborn babies are perfect examples. There have been many studies and books written about the benefits of proper abdominal breathing. The diaphragm (a layer of muscle in the abdomen, in the waist area) is used in this technique and related meditative and breathing methods. It is also used in many traditional martial arts, and is associated with and responsible for incredible physical abilities. If you ever watched a demonstration of genuine Shaolin Monks, then you know exactly to what I refer. Again, one may go into great detail, but for the full understanding of the Dan Tian breathing technique, you only need to know this:

- Keep your focus on your Dan Tian (with or without the help of your thumb).
- Touch the upper palate with the tip of your tongue and keep it there.
- Exhale all the air out of your lungs in order to prepare.
- Slowly start breathing in through your nose.
- Push out your abdomen slowly, allowing the lower part of your lungs to be filled with fresh air.
- Once your abdomen is completely pushed out (with your diaphragm pushed downwards), do not continue filling the upper part of lungs with air.
- Slowly exhale through your mouth while squeezing your abdomen and lifting your diaphragm upwards.

There must be no tension or contractions. Your body should be relaxed and your mind calm, focused on Dan Tian and breathing. As much as you apply and pay attention to this deep breathing technique and your Dan Tian, it will gradually become more and more natural to you. You must get into the attentive mood of this relaxed and deep abdominal breathing while resting the attention of your mind on the main energy center of your body – your Dan Tian.

Very soon, you will find yourself breathing in this way any time that you feel some sort of energy imbalance around you (stress, fear, lack of energy).

3. '8 Moons'

This method is one of the easiest and most loved by Chi Meditation practitioners, even among those who are experienced. The main reason is probably because of the range of benefits enjoyed as soon the method is understood and applied in the right way. This Chi Meditation exercise is basically helped by breathing, and is called the 'Beauty of 8 Moons'.

As you may know, the goal of working with Chi is to improve energy flow within the body. In order to better understand that point, we can use the following example. Chi is like water, while Chi Meditation is similar to methods of dealing with the force of water (such as found in strong river currents).

In the same way that you cannot control the force of the water, but you can control the direction of the river's flow in various ways, Chi Meditation will allow your mind to direct the chi energy from one region of your body to another region. The meridians in the body (the paths of energy flow) are very much like the river paths in nature, which "channel" or direct the flow of water. In the same way, meridians all over our bodies direct the flow of chi.

That explains the main problem with being sick, weak, or under stress and tension. Anything which blocks the meridians of the body lowers the intensity of energy flow and creates disharmony in our microcosmic system. When the meridians are not able to "channel" enough energy needed for proper functioning of all different parts of the body, especially to the main organs, that causes a chain reaction of health problems and disorders. Just like a house made of playing cards, if proper action is not taken, everything gradually but surely collapses.

Technique:

The best would be to do this exercise in the morning and then in the evening before you go to sleep, but you can do it during the day as well. This is essentially the exercise that will teach you how to control the flow of Chi by proper focus of attention and breathing. It ensures that the energy within us will flow naturally and has an immediate calming effect.

Three Levels of Breathing

Generally speaking, there are three different levels of breathing. Start with the first and gradually progress via the second to the third level of the 8 Moons, having your entire attention focused on your breath:

1. *First level* - breathe softly so the person standing next to you cannot hear you.

2. *Second level* - breathe softly so that you do not hear yourself breathing.

3. *Third level* - breathe so softly that you do not feel that you are breathing.

The word <u>softly</u> is in the main focus – you should be continuously breathing but not holding your breath. Breathe softly and gently, going from the first to the third level as explained above. It may sound too simple, but once you start doing it, you will see it has a very strong effect of breathing on the third level, which is the purpose of the exercise.

The goal is to completely relax, breathing so softly that you do not feel your own breathing. The key to staying awake and alert (especially if you are tired while exercising) is to keep your attention on further calming your breath. It is not an oxymoron – when you get to stage three, you will know it.

When you practice, keep your spine straight, regardless of your posture (sitting, standing up, or lying down). Relax as much you can. Calm your mind and focus on your breathing pattern. Have your tongue touch the upper palate at all times during the exercise.

Breathing this softly, especially in the beginning, might seem uncomfortable. Sometimes you will find that you are holding your breath. Just relax and start over. Don't hold your breath. Don't force your body to do something your body doesn't want to do.

Practice it every day if you can. If not, do it at least four to five times during the week, because an occasional practice session will not benefit you enough. Try to do it even twice or three times per day. Be sure that if you do, it will be much more beneficial, and you will experience relief much faster.

Most people practice this exercise in the mornings. The reason for that is the simple and convenient fact that energy in the morning is much more fresh than during any other point of the day. So, the best and most beneficial thing will be to start the day with a Chi Meditation exercise, moving Chi in your body in healthy but powerful ways, so your whole day can go smoothly. As time passes, you will notice stress decreasing slowly but surely.

Great masters do recommend doing this exercise in the evening as well, especially if you feel very weak, have a great lack of energy, or if you have trouble sleeping. If you can, you should practice 8 Moons in the evening to get rid of all the tensions accumulated during the day. This Chi practice should be like a nurturing light meal. We all need food and water in order to live, but we shouldn't neglect the fact that we live on Chi. In the same way that we eat when we are hungry, we should practice whenever we need Chi in our body.

When we don't, what do you think will happen?

Chapter V. – Maximize Your Chi

Traditional Chi Kung (Qi Gong) is a very profound science. It covers many different kinds of meditation practices and ways to move and use Chi energy. The first advanced techniques taught by most of the masters are the Little Cycle Universe (Xiao Zhou Tian) and the Large Cycle Universe (Da Zhou Tian).

1. 'Little Universe' Micro Cycle

The Small Micro Cycle meditation is situated at the very beginning of the advanced study material. As soon you feel comfortable with the previously explained techniques, you can start learning about and practicing Little Universe. As we already explained, the life energy of Chi is constantly traveling throughout the body in cycles using the paths of energy – meridians. The excellence of this creation can be perceived through the complexity of the meridians and how our body (or micro universe) is managed. It is very complex and, you can believe me or not, one can study it throughout a whole lifetime. So, what is the Little Universe Micro Cycle technique all about?

Map of Ren and Du Meridian

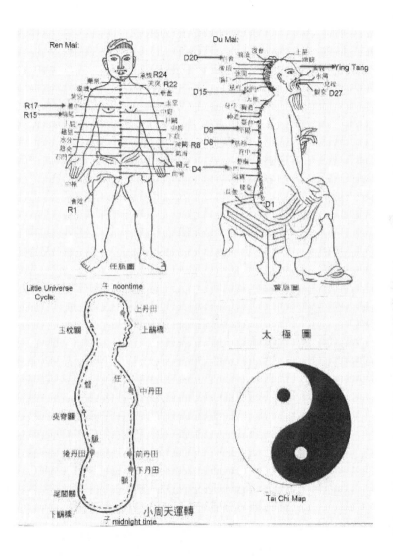

One should know a bit more in order to understand this matter in full. I do not say that you need to engage in a profound study, though the power of the following truth must be acknowledged:

"In addition to'how', if you understand the reason and the benefit of what you get, you will perform any type of inner or physical action to reach complete success much more quickly..."

2. Du Meridian:

Let's start with one common bit of misinformation about the beginning of the Du meridian. It is important to know that this meridian isn't located anywhere on the surface of the body, as many inexperienced 'teachers' and 'experts' explain. Its roots lie deep within the lower abdomen (i.e. in the area of the lower Dan Tian). It shows up on the surface of the body at the spot known as DU1 (located at the root of the spine, just in the middle distance between the tip of the coccyx and the anus) and then ascends along the midline of the sacrum, and through the interior of the spine.

At the nape of the neck, one part enters the brain and emerges at the DU20 point known as *Bai Hui*, at the very tip or crown of the head. There is another branch of the Du meridian that continues around the back area of the skull and finally merges with first branch. From the crown of the head, the channel descends along the midline of the forehead and nose to its final point, DU26, at the junction of the upper lip and gum. As with most meridians, Du has few secondary branches. For example, one of them begins in the lower abdomen (the same as the primary meridian branch), then circles the external genitalia, ascends to the navel region, continues to spread through the heart, travels around the mouth area, and finally splits to ascend the lower border of the two eyes.

There are other branches as well, all spreading around the most important areas of the organs and nerves around the spine.

3. Ren Meridian:

Like the Du meridian, the Ren meridian doesn't begin outside on the surface of the body. In female bodies, it originates in the area of the uterus, while it's found in male bodies in the lower abdomen. It emerges on the surface of the body at *Hui Yin* in the perineum area. From there it ascends along the midline of the abdomen, chest, throat and jaw, ending at the point Ren24, just below the lower lip. An internal portion of the channel then circles the mouth, touching with the DU26 point situated above the upper lip and finally ascending to ST1, just below the eye. There is a part of the Ren that begins in the pelvic area, right after enters into the spine and ascends to the base of the skull and lower jaw. This particular branch runs basically parallel with the Du meridian points and so it facilitates the mutual interdependence between these two main Chi energy pathways:

Ren - the strongest Yin of all meridians and

Du - the strongest Yang of all meridians.

Another secondary branch of the Ren meridian travels along the midline of the front side of the torso, providing full access to the most important internal organs. Its uniqueness is also in the ability to easily nourish the lower Dan Tian, the storehouse of the body's deepest types of energies.

When manipulated with success, just as in the proper use of the Little Universe Micro Cycle, one can achieve extraordinary effects. How is that - and why? Are you interested?

Normally, in the bodies of average men and women, Chi cycles slowly. Other channels, especially two main meridians (Du & Ren), facilitate Chi flow at a speed of about one cycle per day. Chi Meditation masters can make it faster, with speed increasing at more advanced levels. Speed or frequency doubles in about 4 to 8 weeks of practice on average. Later it speeds up even more, and a person can reach the level when Chi takes only one minute to complete a circle or even only 30 seconds! Why that is so extraordinary?

4. 'Little Universe' Micro Cycle - Meditation

Why?

The previously explained theory, despite its necessity and interesting content, doesn't fully explain *why we practice* this Little Universe meditation question. While there is a long list of the benefits achieved by successful practice of this method, ancient masters explain that Little Universe Meditation *'rejuvenates each and every part of the physical and mental body'*.

One may think this explanation is just too simple, or that is just 'unrealistic' to expect recovery and energy recharge / rejuvenation of all parts of the physical and mental body by practicing a single method of meditation. Well, that is why one has to form a complete picture. If you recall, I previously explained that normally, Chi cycles your main meridians about one cycle per day. You move, breathe, think, and work with that one cycle of Chi per day. What do you think will happen to your muscles and bones, organs, brain, and bodily functions when you get your Chi cycles to circulate two, three, or twenty times quicker? Yes, you are right – the only logical and truthful answer is that 'everything improves'. If you want to reload your life force, recharge and rejuvenate your energy level, stay healthy, kill diseases, boost your stamina and focus, (thus greatly improving your performance in practically every area of life) you need to learn this method correctly.

How?

1. PREPARE: By now, you will be well accustomed to the best and fastest ways to prepare mind, body, and environment for meditation. Please do not skip over working through all of the necessary steps of preparation. Even if you feel that you do not need to prepare well for your meditation anymore, you will gain a lot more if you do prepare, as much you can.

2. SIT UP STRAIGHT: A sitting position with a straight spine is normally better than a standing position, especially in the beginning while you are learning the technique. However, it's really up to your preference. You do not need any special meditative sitting position or anything like that. The only thing that is truly important is keeping your spine straight, either sitting

on a straight-backed chair or some comfortable style of sitting on the ground.

3. TENSIONS CHECK: Close your eyes and check if there are any unnecessary tensions that remain somewhere in your body. Most importantly, check and get rid of the tension of the muscles on the face, neck, jaw, and shoulder area.

4. CHI BREATHING: Start with Chi breathing as described in the previous chapter. In order to get the best possible results and quickly advance in Little Universe Meditation, you should be very comfortable with the Chi breathing technique by now.

5. DIAMOND PALMS: Put your palms on the lower abdomen area. There are a few positions used when practicing, but the preferred way (loved by most practitioners) is to place the palms in a shape that resembles a triangle or diamond. You get 'diamond palms' when the tips of the thumbs are touching directly over your navel, and your first fingers are touching a few inches below the navel. Your palms will

form a triangle shape (or diamond-like shape) with your Dan Tian in the middle.

6. GOLDEN CHI: As you probably know, Chi energy (in its purest form) is available everywhere around us. Switch on your visualization, and with your mind's eye, imagine that you are breathing in golden light that travels via the Ren or Du meridian. That gives you two options for seeing the path, which is traveled by the liquid golden Chi or golden bright light, from the direction of your nose toward your lower abdomen. With each breath you take, feel and see the movement of the golden Chi. From your nose, golden light travels across the middle of your body, down to your Dan Tian, and out between your palms and fingers.

7. CHARGING the DAN TIAN: Imagine that with each breath, that golden bright light fills the space of your Dan Tian. See how with each breathing cycle, the amount and concentration of the beautiful golden-white light grows and expands, forming a sphere of energy. With each inhalation, the power and intensity of this golden sphere of light gets bigger and stronger. As you do this,

you may feel a sensation of warmth or tingling, or possibly chills. Relax and do not fight these sensations – enjoy them. This charging part of the exercise will last through a minimum of 9 breath cycles. 27 cycles is the optimal number, at least for beginners. Sometimes you may feel that your energy is very strong and you do not need to do this step, but do it anyway, at least for the recommended duration of 9 cycles.

8. DETECT the HUI YIN: There is a simple method that will help you to detect *Hui Yin*. After a while, you won't feel the need to use this step and you may soon realize that this is a 'crouch-like' process. However, you can be sure it is absolutely needed until you are able to perform step 9 without this step 8. So, using your thumb or middle finger of the left hand (if you are a man) or right hand (if you are a woman), find and press on the Hui Yin for the duration of a few breathing cycles. Where can it be found? Hui Yin is the first point on the Ren meridian – it is located about a half-inch in front of the anus. In male bodies, it is exactly behind the root of the scrotum, while on female bodies, it is found just behind the posterior labial commissure. Pressure should be painful but it shouldn't

cause you any sort of lasting discomfort. You should only use it to clarify the location of *Hui Yin* and so become ready for step 9.

9. HUI YIN 1: Once you feel that your Dan Tian is charged with powerful golden Chi, you can proceed toward the next step. Just as described in step 7, breathe in the golden light and direct it towards the powerful Chi sphere in your Dan Tian. Now, when you exhale, simply direct that sphere of golden energy from the Dan Tian area downwards to the Hui Yin point. Use the power of your imagination combined with a clear intention. This step is natural, and Chi will 'listen'and bend to your desire. Simply move the energy in this way. It will happen. With the next breath, proceed to the next step without repeating this action.

10.UP TOWARDS THE CROWN: This time when you inhale, you visualize (and feel) that golden bright sphere of powerful Chi now in your *Hui Yin*, immediately being drawn upwards. As you start inhaling, see how the golden Chi sphere "bounces" upwards off of the *Hui Yin* into the lower end of the spine. With intent and attention, allow (with a single inhalation) the sphere of golden bright light to flow up, all the way from the root of the spine to the center of your brain, directly beneath the crown of the head. As you exhale, proceed to the last step.

11.WATERFALL: While you exhale, feel how energy starts flowing from the crown of your head, just like a waterfall, downwards across the middle of your face and torso, right back in the direction of your Dan Tian.

Congratulations, you have just completed your 1st Little Universe micro cycle.

Final Guidelines:

Normally, every student enjoys the practice. If there are difficulties, most of the time they are reported on steps 9, 10 or 11. Those key steps of the 'Little Universe' cycle meditation (steps 9-11) are done in a row and soon will become very natural to you. Though this difficulty may not be part of your experience, while you learn this method, you may feel your mind wander off while your attention span weakens. If that occurs, it will help you to rest a bit from steps 9-11 and continue accumulating fresh Chi in the golden energy sphere of your Dan Tian (step 7).

Rest for few breath cycles, before again moving to step 9 and further, moving energy down to *Hui Yin*, up along the spine to the brain and then again downward, across the front of the body back to your Dan Tian. As you get more experienced, your ability to move the Chi will grow and expand and you will know it. There is no need to guess - you do not need anything else for perfecting the Little Universe meditation.

Just as in any inner discipline, mindset and attitude both play significant roles in in any type of Chi Meditation. You should not only be aware of this fact, but also do your best to maintain it at all times while you practice.

Also, keep a gentle focus. You have to be aware and concentrate yet without the compulsive mental spasm of"I must do it now"or any similar thoughts. You are focused but in gentle, soft, and playful manner.

If you notice yourself clenching, in any way (either physically or mentally), and you can't continue even to step 7, then simply take a break – stop your practice entirely. Sometimes those pauses are needed and those may for a few minutes or even longer if you feel the need. You should return to your meditation with the freshness and rejuvenated spirit of childlike playfulness and patience.

After a little bit of practice, you *will advance quickly* and start enjoying the benefits of Chi meditation, one after another. As I promised in the beginning of this book, your health (physical, mental, and emotional) will mold into a natural *harmonious form of unity*. Chi meditation will rejuvenate your existence on all levels, because everything around us and within us is driven by Chi energy. The causes of pain and discomfort, and all that stops us from living better and full lives will gradually melt down. Blockages will disappear, and you will feel the full freedom and power of living in harmony with Chi and with the universe.

Feel free to contact Sifu William Lee at sifu.william.lee@gmail.com

Check out his Amazon profile at http://www.amazon.com/William-Lee/e/B00DWFOCV8/

Next Steps

Please, write me an honest review about the book – I truly value your opinion and thoughts and I will incorporate them into my next book, which is already being prepared.

Leave your review of my book on the Kindle page at
https://www.amazon.com/5-Minute-Stress-Management-Tension-Killers-ebook/dp/B00DYXLD9W

THANK YOU!

More Great and Helpful Books Authored

By Sifu William Lee

Author of Amazon Bestsellers:

5-Minute Chi Boost

5- Minute Stress Management

T.A.E. Total Attack Elimination

Happy & Gluten Free

Chi Healing Powers Book Set

Total Self Defense Book Set

&

Total Chi Fitness

Copyright and Disclaimer

Made in the USA
San Bernardino, CA
09 February 2018